How Far Is It?

Ilse Battistoni

Rosen Classroom Books & Materials
New York

Published in 2003 by The Rosen Publishing Group, Inc.
29 East 21st Street, New York, NY 10010

Book Design: Ron A. Churley

Photo Credits: Cover (background), pp. 1 (background), 6–7, 8 (ruler and scale), 11, 12, 14 by Ron A. Churley; cover (inset), p. 1 (inset) © Jim Pickerell/Stock Connection/PictureQuest; p. 4 © Robert Brenner/PhotoEdit/PictureQuest; p. 8 (top inset) © Britt Erlanson/The Image Bank.

ISBN: 0-8239-6377-2
6-pack ISBN: 0-8239-9559-3

Manufactured in the United States of America

Contents

4

A Look at Maps

A map is a drawing of a place. Maps can tell you many things. You can look at a map of the place where you live to find your street or your school. You can look at a map to find out where a town or city is. Maps can tell you where rivers, lakes, and oceans are, too.

Have you ever looked at a map of the United States? Can you find where you live?

What Is a Key?

Maps have something on them called a **key**. A map's key tells you what the pictures or signs on the map stand for. A map's key might help you find where mountains and forests are on the map.

Look at the pictures in the key. You can use these pictures to find the mountains and forests on the map.

Pacific Ocean

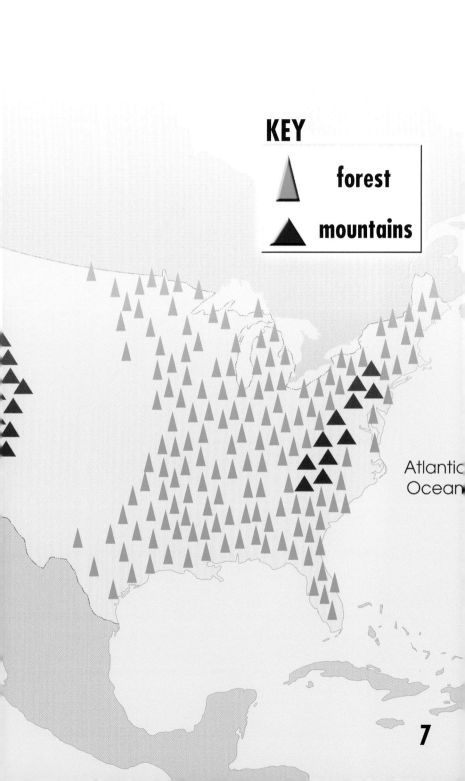

KEY

▲ forest

▲ mountains

Atlantic
Ocean

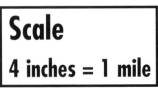

Scale
4 inches = 1 mile

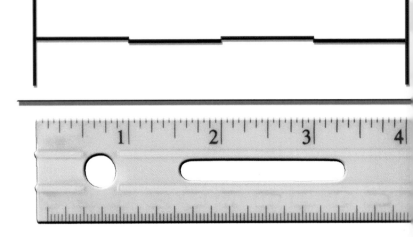

What Is a Scale?

Some maps also have a **scale**. A scale helps you **measure** how far it is from one place to another place. First, you use a ruler to measure the scale. Then you use your ruler and the map to find out how far it is from place to place.

Most maps have scales that can be measured in inches. In this scale, four inches stands for one mile.

How Far Is It?

Use this map's scale to find out how far it is from the pond to the school. First, look at the scale. On this map, two inches **equals** (EE-kwulz) one mile. Find two inches on your ruler. Now use your ruler to measure how far it is from the pond to the school.

On the map, the pond and the school are two inches apart. That means that the pond and the school are one mile apart.

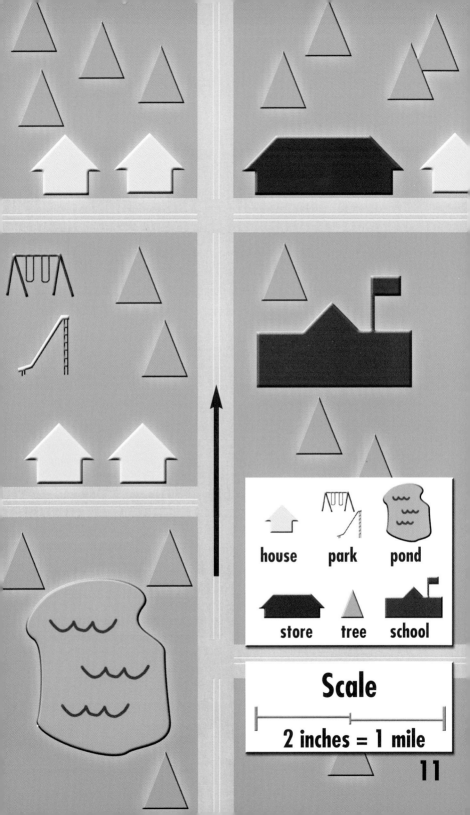

house   park   pond

store   tree   school

Scale

2 inches = 1 mile

11

house   park   pond

store   tree   school

Scale

2 inches = 1 mile

12

A Trip to the Store

Now look at the map to find out how far it is from the pond to the store. Look at the scale again. Use your ruler to measure how far it is from the pond to the store. On this map, the pond and the store are four inches apart.

The scale says that two inches equals one mile, so four inches equals two miles. It is two miles from the pond to the store.

A Walk to the Park

How far would you have to walk to get from the school to the park? Use your ruler to measure how far apart they are on the map. They are only two inches apart. That means you would only have to walk one mile to get from the school to the park!

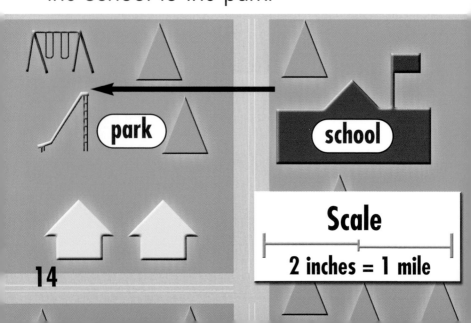

park

school

Scale

2 inches = 1 mile